★ *GREAT SPORTS TEAMS* ★

THE PHILADELPHIA

76ERS

BASKETBALL TEAM

Glen Macnow

Enslow Publishers, Inc.

44 Fadem Road   PO Box 38
Box 699   Aldershot
Springfield, NJ 07081 Hants GU12 6BP
USA   UK

Library of Congress Cataloging-in-Publication Data

Macnow, Glen.
    The Philadelphia 76ers basketball team / Glen Macnow.
        p. cm. — (Great sports teams)
    Includes bibliographical references (p.) and index.
    Summary: A team history of the City of Brotherly Love's sports franchise whose star players and coaches include Julius Erving, Wilt Chamberlain, Alex Hannum, Moses Malone, and Charles Barkley.
    ISBN 0-7660-1063-5
    1. Philadelphia 76ers (Basketball team)—History—Juvenile literature.
[1. Philadelphia 76ers (Basketball team)—History. 2. Basketball—History.]
I. Title. II. Series.
GV885.52.P45M33 1998
796.323'64'0974811—dc21   97-20378
                                                 CIP
                                                 AC

Printed in the United States of America

10 9 8 7 6 5 4 3 2 1

Illustration Credits: AP/Wide World Photos, pp. 4, 7, 8, 10, 13, 14, 16, 19, 20, 22, 25, 26, 28, 31, 32, 34, 37, 38.

Cover Illustration: AP/Wide World Photos.

CONTENTS

1 The 1982–83 Team 5

2 History of the Sixers 11

3 Players 17

4 Coaches 23

5 The 1966–67 Team 29

6 Looking to the Future 35

Statistics 40

Chapter Notes 43

Glossary 45

Further Reading 46

Index 47

Where to Write 48

*S*urrounded by Boston Celtics, Moses Malone tosses a hook shot over the outstretched arm of Larry Bird.

THE 1982-83 TEAM

The 1982 National Basketball Association (NBA) season ended sadly for the Philadelphia 76ers. After finishing the season with 58 wins and cruising through the first three rounds of the playoffs, the team had hopes of winning the title. Yet the Los Angeles Lakers ended that dream, beating the Sixers—four games to two—in the NBA Finals.

Afterward, surrounded by reporters in the locker room, Sixers star Julius Erving had a message for Philadelphia fans. "Tell them that we owe them one," he said.[1]

That statement became the motto for the next season: "We owe you one." Call it a promise. And the Sixers delivered.

Rarely does a team dedicate a season to its fans. Yet in Philly, the players appreciated the support they got. The Sixers had not won a title since 1967, but the fans kept coming to the Spectrum to cheer their team.

Delivering the Promise

What a team it was! The 1982–83 Sixers were led by Erving—"Doctor J" to his fans—a high-flying superstar who could defy gravity. One guard was Andrew Toney, a bull's-eye shooter. The other was Maurice "Mo" Cheeks, a smart, steady player who could pass the ball through the eye of a needle. Bobby Jones provided defense and hustle. And a mountain of a man named Moses Malone grabbed most of the rebounds at center.

As the NBA playoffs started in 1983, Malone gave his prediction as to how many games he thought it would take for the Sixers to win the title.

"Four, four, four,"[2] he said. In other words, they would sweep three straight best-of-seven series without a loss.

Actually, it took them four, five, and four to win it all. Yet in the end, the 1983 Sixers swept the Lakers in a rematch. They kept the promise that Erving had made to Philadelphia fans. The Philadelphia 76ers were the NBA champions!

On June 2, 1983, two million Sixers fans crowded along a parade route on Broad Street in Philadelphia. They cheered crazily when Erving stood at City Hall and said, "Now that we've done it once, let's do it again. Let's make winning a habit."[3]

Unfortunately, it was not to be. The Sixers remained one of the NBA's top teams through the 1980s, but never again won a title. Indeed, in the long history of the franchise, there have been only two NBA championships.

The Philadelphia 76ers Basketball Team

Sixers point guard Maurice Cheeks lays a shot over Michael Jordan of the Chicago Bulls.

Some Exciting Moments

That does not mean that things have not been exciting. The history of the Philadelphia 76ers is one of the most interesting in sports. Two of their squads—the 1983 team and an earlier one in 1967—are still regarded among the all-time greatest in basketball history. On the flip side, the 1972–73 team was

Though not a member of Philadelphia's championship teams, "Sir" Charles Barkley provided many highlights for 76ers fans.

probably the worst ever to suit up. That club won just nine games and lost 73. At one point, they lost an NBA-record 20 games in a row.

Some of the greatest and most colorful players in history have passed through Philly. The first that comes to mind is Wilt Chamberlain, a giant from the 1960s, who still owns more records than any other player. Other Hall of Famers who have played for the 76ers include Erving, NBA pioneer Dolph Schayes, point guard Hal Greer, and Billy Cunningham—who was both a great player and coach for the club. Add in future NBA Hall of Famers Malone and Charles Barkley, and you can see the excitement the Sixers have brought to their fans over the years.

_____

Future Stars

In recent times, there has been less excitement. The club suffered through six straight losing seasons in the 1990s. Now it seems like help is on the way for Philadelphia. In the 1996 draft, the 76ers chose Allen Iverson from Georgetown University with the first overall pick. Iverson came to Philly with as much pure speed as any player in the game and a crossover dribble that was unstoppable.

When Iverson joined the Sixers, he made a pledge to the city. It may take a few years, he said, but the NBA championship trophy would return to Philadelphia. He would bring it back. Like Julius Erving had done years earlier, Iverson intends to keep his promise.[4]

*B*efore moving to Philadelphia, the 76ers were known as the Syracuse Nationals. Dolph Schayes (shown here) was the star player of those Syracuse teams.

HISTORY OF THE SIXERS

The history of pro basketball in Philadelphia actually begins with a team known as the Warriors, who won the first National Basketball Association title in 1947. The league was known then as the Basketball Association of America. The team's star player was "Jumpin' Joe" Fulks, a skinny, self-described hillbilly from Kentucky. Fulks was slow and rarely passed, but he was a great shooter. In the NBA's first season, he averaged 23.2 points per game—nearly seven more than the league's next-best scorer.[1]

The Warriors won another title in 1956. This time, the star was Paul Arizin, a home-grown player from nearby Villanova University. Arizin played despite a sinus condition that made him wheeze. His wheezing may have been loud, but he sure could shoot.

Despite that success, the Warriors did not make much money. In 1962, the franchise packed up and moved to San Francisco. Philadelphia fans were left without an NBA team.

Schayes and the Nationals

One year later, wealthy local businessmen Irv Kosloff and Isaac Richman came to the rescue. They bought the struggling Syracuse Nationals and moved the team from New York to Philly.[2] That team came with a star—center Dolph Schayes. One of the best all-around players in history, Schayes specialized in driving to the basket and drawing a foul for a three-point play. He was also a great passer and rebounder. And Schayes did not miss a game in more than ten seasons—playing 764 straight. Before baseball had Cal Ripken, Jr., basketball had Dolph Schayes.

Most of Schayes's early NBA records have been broken by the likes of Michael Jordan and Kareem Abdul-Jabbar. Yet in his time, he was the best.

In their early years, the 76ers were a very good team. But they never were good enough to beat the Boston Celtics. From the late 1950s through the mid-60s, the Celtics won eight NBA titles in a row. Most years, the Sixers (or before them, the Nats) finished second.

Help Arrives

Schayes retired as a player in 1964, but stayed in Philly to coach the Sixers. In 1965, he helped pull off one of the greatest trades in franchise history. He swapped three average players for Wilt Chamberlain. Maybe Chamberlain—known as "Wilt the Stilt" or

*W*ilt Chamberlain skies for the rebound against Walt Bellamy of the New York Knicks. Trading for Chamberlain was one of the best moves in Philadelphia's history.

Hal Greer was one of the leading scorers on Alex Hannum's Philadelphia teams of the late 1960s.

"the Big Dipper"—would be the player who helped the Sixers catch the Celtics.

Philadelphia fans already knew Chamberlain quite well. He grew up in town and starred in basketball, track, and football at Overbrook High School. His speed, power, and coordination had some experts thinking he was the best athlete in the world.[3]

Chamberlain played for the Warriors for three seasons before their move to San Francisco. As a rookie in 1959–60, he led the league in scoring and was voted Most Valuable Player. In one game in 1962, he grabbed 55 rebounds, still an NBA record. That same season, he scored 100 points in a single game. No other player has ever come within 27 of that mark.

Chamberlain was hailed as a hero when he returned to Philadelphia in 1965. The team finished ahead of the Celtics in the regular season that year, but still lost to Boston in the playoffs. Days later, Coach Schayes retired, saying, "I have every reason to believe this team can be the next [group of] champions."[4]

He sure was right. Alex Hannum was hired to replace Schayes, and the team he inherited may have been the best in NBA history. Hannum preached teamwork—passing the ball, finding the open man— rather than the star system the Sixers had played. He sold the idea to Chamberlain. The result was fewer points for Chamberlain, but more assists, rebounds, and blocked shots. With a potent team from top to bottom, the Sixers finished with a record of 68 wins and just 13 losses. Not until the 1995–96 Chicago Bulls did any team win more games in a season.

The Sixers then mowed down the hated Boston Celtics in five games. And they beat San Francisco— Chamberlain's old team—in the Finals. Chamberlain and the 76ers had won their first NBA title.

*W*ilt Chamberlain fights for a loose ball with Bill Russell of the Boston Celtics. Almost everyone agrees that Chamberlain and Russell are among the best centers in NBA history.

PLAYERS

One of America's greatest monuments is Mount Rushmore in South Dakota. Carved into a mountain, and visible from 90 miles away, are the faces of four great United States presidents—Washington, Jefferson, Lincoln, and Theodore Roosevelt.

If the Philadelphia 76ers ever carved a Mount Rushmore of their all-time greats, it would feature Wilt Chamberlain, Julius Erving, Moses Malone, and Charles Barkley. And what a monument it would be.

Wilt Chamberlain

Start with Chamberlain. Most people growing up in the 1990s regard Michael Jordan as the best player of all time. Ask someone who grew up in the 1960s or '70s. Chances are, you'll hear "the Big Dipper."

Chamberlain was a Goliath—seven-feet one-inch and 290 pounds—when there were few players of that size. He was durable—once averaging more than 48 minutes per game for an entire season. And he was smart. Not once in his fourteen-year career did he foul out of a game. He led the league in rebounding ten times and in scoring seven times. He was such a dominant player in his day that the league changed rules to make things more even. One change barred him from leaping from the foul line while shooting foul shots and dunking the ball before ever touching the ground. Since then, players have had to stay entirely behind the line.

"If Michael Jordan played in my time," Chamberlain once said, "he would not come through the middle for all those fancy dunks. If he tried it, I would knock him flat on his back."[1]

Julius Erving

If Chamberlain was a circus giant, Julius Erving was the NBA's greatest acrobat.

Known as "the Doctor" or "Dr. J," Erving was one of the first players to become famous for flying above the rim. His unique moves—thunder dunks and reverse layups—were the result of hours and hours of practice as a boy growing up outside of New York City. No player ever could bring a crowd to its feet like "the Doctor."

Erving came to the 76ers in a 1976 trade with the New Jersey Nets. The trade cost the Sixers three players and $6 million, but it was worth it. "Dr. J is a once-in-a-lifetime player," said General Manager Pat Williams.[2]

That season, the Sixers won their first Eastern Division title in a decade. They lost to Portland in the

The Philadelphia 76ers Basketball Team

nown as Dr. J, Julius Erving dazzled fans everywhere with his spectacular dunks and scoring moves.

NBA Finals. Indeed, Erving kept the Sixers at or near the top of the standings during his eleven seasons there. He made the All-Star Team every single year he played pro ball.

Moses Malone

Even with Erving, the great Sixers' teams of the 1970s and '80s seemed one player short of winning a title. The position they needed to fill was center. The man who filled it was Moses Malone.

The 76ers' Charles Barkley looks to pull a rebound away from Reggie Lewis of Boston.

Malone, a six-foot ten-inch wide-body, was a star before he set foot in Philadelphia. He won the NBA's Most Valuable Player Award (MVP) in 1982 while playing for the Houston Rockets. Houston's owner was going broke, so he sent Malone to the Sixers for some cash and an average player.[3]

The Philadelphia 76ers Basketball Team

What a move for the Sixers! Malone gave the Sixers the big body they needed in the middle. He was a rebounding machine, leading the NBA six times in that category. And he averaged at least twenty points per game for 11 straight seasons. Although he only played four seasons with the Sixers, he teamed with Erving to form the league's best 1-2 offensive punch. With him, the Sixers won the championship in 1983.

Malone was traded in 1986. By then, the Sixers had found another rebounding and scoring machine— Charles Barkley.

Charles Barkley

As a young man, the chubby Barkley was known as "the Round Mound of Rebound." As he matured, he lost the weight. Yet he never lost his skill at rebounding. Eventually, his nickname became one of respect. Players called him "Sir Charles."

Barkley was a bubbling vat of energy. Although he stood just six feet five inches, he grappled with men nine inches taller for key rebounds. He bounced through the lane to lay up crucial baskets. And he kept running conversations going with opponents, referees, and even fans during games. No player in the NBA has ever shown more personality.

Barkley spent eight years in Philadelphia. In seven of those seasons, he averaged more than twenty points per game. In one of the worst moves ever made by the franchise, he was traded in 1992 to the Phoenix Suns. For the next five seasons, the Sixers' record kept getting worse.

*U*sing an offense that stressed finding the open man, Alex Hannum led the 76ers to their first NBA championship.

COACHES

Just two coaches have won National Basketball Association titles with the Philadelphia 76ers. The first was Alex Hannum in 1967. The second was Billy Cunningham in 1983. These two coaches were as different as a fast break and a four-corner offense. Their success shows how opposite styles can work in the NBA.

Alex Hannum

Hannum was a quiet man and a master of strategy. Long after games had ended, Hannum would sit in his office. Under the light of a single desk lamp, he would diagram plays and design new defenses. Even today, he is praised as someone who helped design the modern NBA game.

Hannum came to the Sixers in 1966 after coaching the Golden State Warriors. His new squad faced a tough challenge. The Boston Celtics had won the NBA title eight years in a row. How could the 76ers get past Boston?

Hannum preached playing a team game. Sure, the Sixers had the league's top player, Wilt Chamberlain, who had averaged more than 33 points per game the previous season. Yet the Sixers could only be the best if Chamberlain passed a little more and shot a little less, Hannum said.[1] He designed an offense that got all five players involved.

The plan worked. The 1966–67 Sixers, with their balanced offense, were one of the greatest teams in NBA history. They won 68 regular season games and lost just 13. Not until the 1995–96 Chicago Bulls did any team win more games. Hannum's club swept past the Celtics and Warriors in the playoffs to bring Philadelphia its first championship.

"Wilt was our best player, but Coach Hannum was the most valuable member of the team," said Hal Greer, a Hall of Fame guard from that squad. "He convinced us all to swallow our egos and play as a team. He came up with new strategies all the time. And they always worked. He's the best coach I ever played for."[2]

Billy Cunningham

Another one of the important players on that 1966–67 club was Billy Cunningham. A six-feet six-inch burner who switched between guard and forward, Cunningham starred for the Sixers for nine seasons. Coach Hannum taught him to use his head and avoid

The Philadelphia 76ers Basketball Team

*P*hiladelphia coach Billy Cunningham is showered with champagne after his 76ers team defeated the Los Angeles Lakers to win the 1983 NBA title.

making mistakes. Mostly, "Billy C." was loved by Philly fans because of his fire.

"Billy played with as much intensity as anyone I've ever been around," said Luke Jackson, a teammate for seven years on the 76ers. "In a close game, when other guys were scared, you would see a fire in his eyes. He just hated to lose."[3]

As a player, Cunningham was known for his swiftness, aggressiveness, and his weird assortment of shots. He played better and seemed to shoot better when he was bumped by opponents.

O vercome with emotion, the 76ers celebrate their Game 4 victory over the Lakers to win the NBA Championship.

As a coach, Cunningham brought that same emotion to the arena. After retiring as a player, he took over the coaching reigns early in 1978. He stayed for eight seasons, and the Sixers won 70 percent of their games during that era. Each season, they made the playoffs. Three times, they won their division. And in 1983, Cunningham's club won the NBA title.

"Billy C." learned his basketball from Hannum and from legendary coach Dean Smith at the University of North Carolina. Still, he never saw himself as a genius at the game. His coaching strategy was to put his best players on the floor and let them run. If he could inspire them to work hard and have fun, he was doing his job well, he figured.

Did he consider himself a great coach?

"Not at all," Cunningham once said. "If anything, I was smart enough to light a fire under the boys and then just stay out of the way. How great did I have to be to coach Julius Erving and Moses Malone? Honestly, star players can make a coach look pretty smart."[4]

Honestly, Cunningham was too modest. He and Alex Hannum were both great coaches. Their opposite styles show how success can come in different ways.

L ucious Jackson and Hal Greer (#15) succeed in taking the ball away from Bill Russell of the Boston Celtics.

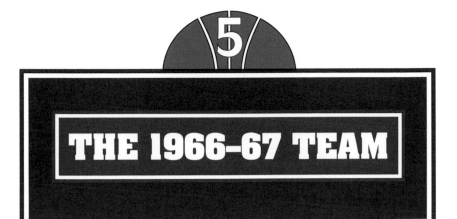

THE 1966–67 TEAM

When pro basketball experts debate which team was the best in history, only a few clubs are worthy of mention. One is Michael Jordan's great Chicago Bulls of the 1990s. Another is the Boston Celtics of the 1980s, led by superstar Larry Bird. Several Los Angeles Lakers' squads over the years are worth considering.

There is one team that may be better than all of them. That team is the Philadelphia 76ers of 1966–67.

Coached by Alex Hannum, that team opened the season in the brand-new Philadelphia Spectrum. Everyone expected the club to be solid that season, maybe even battling with the reigning champions, the Boston Celtics. No one expected them to be as good as they turned out.

A Great Start

The Sixers won their first seven games in 1966. By December, they were an astonishing 26–3—a few games ahead of the Celtics. They then won 13 in a row to go to 39–3. Still, the Celtics, led by center Bill Russell, stayed close in the standings.

Wilt Chamberlain, of course, was the star of this team. Although he shot less often in 1966–67—Coach Hannum's plan—he still averaged 24 points per game. He also averaged 24 rebounds per game, best in the league. He set a shooting accuracy record, making 68 percent of his field goal attempts. He also broke the NBA record for assists by a center.

By spreading the ball around, the Sixers were able to score from all angles. The team's floor captain was guard Hal Greer. He led the team in assists and finished second in scoring. At age thirty-one, Greer was thought by some to be too old to keep up with the fast pace of pro basketball. He said, "I must be fast. Always quick. The day I slow down, I'm finished."[1]

The Supporting Cast

The rest of the team was made up of role players. Each knew he was not a star, but each devoted 100 percent to doing his job to help the team. Forwards Chet Walker and Lucious Jackson focused on playing defense and helping with the rebounds. Guard Wali Jones shot from the outside, and also kept teammates loose with his sense of humor. And reserve Billy Cunningham kept coming off the bench to make clutch shots.

The lesson players learned that season was that sometimes a team plays better when its superstar shines a little less brightly. By sacrificing his own

Billy Cunningham stops in an attempt to fake out Mike Riordan of the Washington Bullets.

goals, Chamberlain gave his teammates a chance to show their talents. Every man contributed to the success. It not only made the Sixers a tougher team to stop, it also made them come together as a unit.

"I learned more about being a man that season than any other time in my life," Greer said. "It was one time when we all worked for the good of the

*F*orward Chet Walker was an important part of the 1967 championship team.

team. If I had a bad night, maybe scored just five points, it didn't matter as long as the team won. We all believed that."[2]

Stopping the Celtics

The Sixers finished the regular season with 68 wins and just 13 losses, at the time the best in NBA history. They were eight games ahead of the Celtics. Yet Boston had pride—and had won 8 straight championships.

The two great squads met in the playoffs. In one game, Chamberlain snared 41 rebounds—a playoff record. In another, he had 16 assists, while Greer scored 35 points. It took five games—four wins and a loss—for the Sixers to dethrone the Celtics. They then dispatched the Golden State Warriors—four games to two—and celebrated their championship.

The elite group of players on the 1966–67 Sixers were never able to repeat their great season. Coach Hannum left after one more season. Chamberlain eventually moved on to the Lakers. But those players—and NBA fans—will never forget that season's Sixers. They may be the best club ever.

"Other teams in history probably had more talent," Greer said. "But no one ever played better as a team. That was what we were all about."[3]

*T*he 76ers selected Jerry Stackhouse with the third pick in the 1995 draft. He led the team in scoring his rookie season.

LOOKING TO THE FUTURE

There is no question that the Philadelphia 76ers fell upon hard times in the 1990s. Each season from 1991–92 to 1995–96 they lost more games than they had the previous season. It was the first time in NBA history that a team's record got worse five years in a row. The team quickly went through five head coaches in little more than five seasons. Nothing seemed to work.

Eventually, things started looking up. The only good thing about finishing at the bottom of the standings is that it gives a team a chance to get the best players coming out of college. The Sixers were ready to make the most of those chances.

New Young Talent

In 1995, the Sixers chose shooting guard Jerry Stackhouse with the third pick in the draft. Stackhouse, from the University of North Carolina, was just twenty years old when he joined the NBA. He quickly showed that he belonged. Playing without much help from a weak collection of teammates, he averaged 19.2 points per game, the best of any NBA rookie that season.

"I love what I see from Jerry Stackhouse," said another one-time University of North Carolina star by the name of Michael Jordan. "He has got the talent and the inner fire to be a dominant player. And, look at him. He's still a baby."[1]

Stackhouse, however, did not figure into the 76ers' long-term plans. The team became concerned that he would not re-sign after the 1997–98 season, and traded him to the Detroit Pistons.

Another Amazing Talent

Another so-called "baby" joined the Sixers in 1996. The Sixers landed the first choice in the draft. They jumped at the chance to pick All-American point guard Allen Iverson from Georgetown University. Iverson was just twenty years old when he played his first NBA game.

Iverson is an amazing talent. His moves are so quick that announcers can't keep up with them. He is so tricky with the ball that cameramen are often faked out. And his joy for the game is so catching that even the tough Philly fans often rise to give him standing ovations.

As a rookie in 1996–97, Iverson averaged more than 20 points per game. And when the NBA's top first-year players got together for their own game

The Philadelphia 76ers Basketball Team

In the 1980s, Maurice Cheeks and Andrew Toney (above) manned Philly's backcourt. Sixers fans hope another star guard, Allen Iverson, can return the team to greatness.

during the league's All-Star weekend, it was Iverson who walked away with the Most Valuable Player award. Said Seattle SuperSonics coach George Karl, "Allen has the tools to be one of the greats in this league. In fact, he probably doesn't know yet how great he can be. It may take him a few years to mature. But when that time comes, he's going to be so good it will be scary."[2]

The Sixers have boasted great backcourt players in the past. In the 1960s, guards Wali Jones and Hal Greer helped bring Philadelphia a title. In the 1980s, Maurice Cheeks brought the ball upcourt and Andrew Toney

*T*he Sixers took Allen Iverson with the top pick in 1996. Iverson went on to be named the 1997 NBA Rookie of the Year.

shot rainbows through the net. Now, as the NBA heads toward the next century, Iverson has the job of restoring glory to the 76ers.

_____

Whatever it Takes

They should have plenty of help. In 1996, the team was sold to a group headed by Pat Croce, the former trainer of the Sixers and a self-proclaimed "maniac about winning."[3] Croce changed nearly everything about the club in his first season—the coach, the general manager, the uniforms, even the team mascot. And he vowed to spend whatever it would take and keep making changes until the 76ers were back on top of the standings.

President John F. Kennedy once referred to Philadelphia as "our nation's hero factory."[4] Many of those heroes have played basketball. From Wilt Chamberlain to Billy Cunningham to Julius Erving to Charles Barkley, Sixers' fans have been blessed to witness these true superstars. The NBA titles they won are represented by banners hanging from the ceiling at the CoreStates Center in Philadelphia.

Now, with Allen Iverson leading the charge, the Sixers are determined to win another NBA crown. Perhaps some day soon, another championship banner will hang above the Sixers' home court.

STATISTICS

Team Record

The 76ers History

YEARS	LOCATION	W	L	PCT	CHAMPIONSHIPS
1946–47—1949–50	Syracuse	136	95	.589	None
1950–51—1959–60	Syracuse	398	312	.561	1955
1960–61—1969–70	Syracuse Philadelphia*	483	323	.599	1967
1970–71—1979–80	Philadelphia	402	418	.490	None
1980–81—1989–90	Philadelphia	529	291	.645	1983
1990–91—1996–97	Philadelphia	194	380	.338	None

*Prior to the 1963–64 season, the Syracuse Nationals moved to Philadelphia and changed their name to the 76ers.

The 76ers Today

SEASON	SEASON RECORD	PLAYOFF RECORD	COACH	DIVISION FINISH
1990–91	44–38	4–4	Jim Lynam	2nd
1991–92	35–47	—	Jim Lynam	5th
1992–93	26–56	—	Doug Moe Fred Carter	6th
1993–94	25–57	—	Fred Carter	6th
1994–95	24–58	—	John Lucas	6th
1995–96	18–64	—	John Lucas	7th
1996–97	22–60	—	Johnny Davis	6th

The Philadelphia 76ers Basketball Team

Total History

SEASON RECORD	PLAYOFF RECORD	NBA CHAMPIONSHIPS
2,142–1,819	179–162	3

Coaching Record

COACH	YEARS COACHED	RECORD	CHAMPIONSHIPS
George Mingin	1946	2–0	None
Benny Borgmann	1946–48	43–59	None
Al Cervi	1948–56	334–224	Eastern Divison, 1950, 1952 NBA Champions, 1955
Paul Seymour	1956–60	155–124	None
Alex Hannum	1960–63 1966–68	257–145	Eastern Division, 1968 NBA Champions, 1967
Dolph Schayes	1963–66	129–111	Eastern Division, 1966
Jack Ramsay	1968–72	174–154	None
Roy Rubin	1972–73	4–47	None
Kevin Loughery	1973	5–26	None
Gene Shue	1973–77	157–177	Atlantic Division, 1977
Billy Cunningham	1977–85	454–196	Atlantic Division, 1978 NBA Champions, 1983
Matt Goukas	1985–88	119–88	None
Jim Lynam	1988–92	194–173	Atlantic Division, 1990
Doug Moe	1992–93	19–37	None
Fred Carter	1993–94	32–76	None
John Lucas	1994–96	42–122	None
Johnny Davis	1996–97	22–60	None

Ten Great 76ers

PLAYER	SEA	YRS	G	REB	AST	BLK	STL	PTS	AVG
				CAREER STATISTICS					
Charles Barkley	1984–91	13	943	11,027	3,743	843	1,520	21,756	23.1
Wilt Chamberlain	1965–68	14	1,045	23,924	4,643	*	*	31,419	30.1
Maurice Cheeks	1978–89	15	1,101	3,088	7,392	294	2,310	12,195	11.1
Doug Collins	1973–81	8	415	1,339	1,368	114	519	7,427	17.9
Billy Cunningham**	1965–72 1974–76	11	770	7,981	3,305	66*	390*	16,310	21.2
Julius Erving**	1976–87	16	1,243	10,525	5,176	1,941*	2,272*	30,026	24.2
Hal Greer	1958–73	15	1,122	5,665	4,540	*	*	21,586	19.2
Allen Iverson	1996–	1	76	312	567	24	157	1,787	23.5
Moses Malone**	1982–86	21	1,455	17,834	1,936	1,733*	1,089*	29,580	20.3
Dolph Schayes	1948–64	17	1,059	11,256*	3,072*	*	*	19,247	18.2

* Statistics are incomplete for some players in some categories. The NBA did not keep statistics on rebounds until 1950–51 and on steals and blocked shots until 1973–74.

**Statistics for these players are their NBA totals combined with their American Basketball Association (ABA) totals.

SEA=Seasons with 76ers
YRS=Years in the NBA
G=Games
REB=Rebounds
AST=Assists

BLK=Blocks
STL=Steals
PTS=Total Points
AVG=Scoring Average

The Philadelphia 76ers Basketball Team

CHAPTER NOTES

Chapter 1
1. Peter C. Bjarkman, *The Encyclopedia of Pro Basketball Team Histories* (New York: Carol & Graf Publishers, Inc., 1994), p. 144.

2. Ibid.

3. Ibid., p. 146.

4. Phil Jasner, "Sixers Rookie Points Way," *Philadelphia Daily News*, September 3, 1996, p. 87.

Chapter 2
1. Robert W. Peterson, *Cages to Jump Shots: Pro Basketball's Early Years* (New York: Oxford University Press, 1990), p. 88.

2. Larry Fox, *Illustrated History of Basketball* (New York: Grosset & Dunlap, 1974), p. 121.

3. Edna and Art Rust, Jr., *Art Rust's Illustrated History of the Black Athlete* (Garden City, N.Y.: Doubleday and Co., Inc., 1985), p. 316.

4. Lou Sabin, *Great Teams of Pro Basketball* (New York: Random House, 1971), p. 44.

Chapter 3
1. Bill Lyon, "Wilt Views Past, Present Through Own Eyes," *Philadelphia Inquirer*, November 11, 1996, p. D1.

2. Tom Peterson, *Philadelphia 76ers* (Mankato, Minn.: Creative Education, Inc., 1989), p. 28.

3. Ibid., p. 40.

Chapter 4
1. Lou Sabin, *Great Teams of Pro Basketball* (New York: Random House, 1971), p. 47.

2. Ibid.

3. Peter C. Bjarkman, *The Encyclopedia of Pro Basketball Team Histories* (New York: Carol & Graf Publishers, Inc., 1994), p. 149.

4. Tom Peterson, *Philadelphia 76ers* (Mankato, Minn.: Creative Education, Inc., 1989), p. 44.

Chapter 5

1. Peter C. Bjarkman, *The Encyclopedia of Pro Basketball Team Histories* (New York: Carol & Graf Publishers, Inc., 1994), p. 145.

2. Ibid.

3. Ibid., p. 146.

Chapter 6

1. Diane Pucin, "One Great Tarheel Praises Another," *Philadelphia Inquirer*, March 23, 1996, p. D1.

2. Phil Jasner, "Despite Early Flaws, Iverson Impresses Coaches," *Philadelphia Daily News*, November 20, 1996.

3. Bill Lyon, "Pat Feels Great—So Do Fans," *Philadelphia Inquirer*, March 13, 1996, p. A1.

4. Tom Peterson, *Philadelphia 76ers* (Mankato, Minn.: Creative Education, Inc., 1989), p. 3.

The Philadelphia 76ers Basketball Team

GLOSSARY

assist—The action (as a throw or pass) of a player who enables a teammate to score a goal.

ballhandling—The ability to control the ball so that the other team will not take it away.

center—This is the Five Man, the team's tallest, and usually strongest player. On many teams, the action of the guards and forwards revolves around the center, trying to get the ball into him for easy inside shots. The center also has to be responsible for rebounding and defense.

driving—In basketball, the act of dribbling the ball toward the basket either to shoot the ball at close range, or draw the defense in so that another teammate becomes open.

fast break offense—A type of offense that calls for a team to try to move the ball quickly upcourt so that they can get easy baskets, mostly dunks or layups.

foul—Illegal physical contact against an opposing player.

four corner offense—An offense that calls for a team to bring the ball up the court slowly, and then have the two guards and two forwards spread out to the four corners of the offensive zone. The center stays in the middle. Often, the ball will be passed around many times before the team tries to pass to someone inside for an easy shot.

point guard—Often referred to as the One Guard. This is the team's lead guard, the player who directs the offense. He handles the ball most of the time, brings it up the court, and delivers it to the man in the best position to shoot it.

rebounding—This is grabbing the ball, shot by a teammate or opponent, that misses and bounces off the rim or backboard.

shooting guard—Also called the Two Guard. This player, usually one of the team's primary scorers, is expected to hit most of his two-point shots and connect with three-pointers.

steal—This occurs when one player is able to take the ball away from the opposing team without having to rebound it.

FURTHER READING

D'Andrea, Joseph C. *If I Were a Philadelphia Seventy-Sixer*. Akron, OH: Picture Me Books, Inc., 1994.

Bjarkman, Peter. *Top 10 Basketball Slam Dunkers*. Springfield, N.J.: Enslow Publishers, Inc., 1995.

Goodman, Michael E. *Philadelphia 76ers*, rev. ed. Mankato, Minn.: Creative Education, Inc., 1993.

Hochman, Stan. *The Sports Book: Everything You Need to Be a Fan in Philadelphia*. Norristown, Pa.: P B Publications, Inc., 1995.

Joseph, Paul. *The Philadelphia 76ers*. Minneapolis, Minn.: Abdo & Daughters Publishing, 1997.

Knapp, Ron. *Top 10 Basketball Scorers*. Springfield, N.J.: Enslow Publishers, Inc., 1994.

Rappoport, Ken. *Top 10 Basketball Legends*. Springfield, N.J.: Enslow Publishers, Inc., 1995.

Sabin, Lou. *Great Teams of Pro Basketball*. New York: Random House, 1971.

Sachare, Alex, ed. *The Official NBA Basketball Encyclopedia*, 2nd ed. New York: Villard Books, 1994.

Savage, Jeff. *Top 10 Basketball Point Guards*. Springfield, N.J.: Enslow Publishers, Inc., 1997.

INDEX

A

Abdul-Jabbar, Kareem, 12
Arizin, Paul, 11

B

Barkley, Charles, 9, 17, 20,
    21, 39
Bird, Larry, 29
Boston Celtics, 12, 15, 23,
    24, 29, 30, 33

C

Chamberlain, Wilt, 9, 12,
    14–15, 17–18, 24, 30, 31,
    39
Cheeks, Maurice, 6, 37
Chicago Bulls, 15, 24, 29
CoreStates Center, 39
Croce, Pat, 39
Cunningham, Billy, 9,
    23–25, 27, 30, 39

E

Erving, Julius, 5, 6, 9,
    17–19, 21, 27, 39

F

Fulks, Joe, 11

G

Georgetown University, 9,
    36
Golden State Warriors, 23,
    24, 33

G

Greer, Hal, 9, 24, 30, 31, 33,
    37

H

Hannum, Alex, 15, 23–24,
    27, 29, 30, 33
Houston Rockets, 20

I

Iverson, Allen, 9, 36–37, 39

J

Jackson, Lucious "Luke,"
    25, 30
Jefferson, Thomas, 17
Jones, Bobby, 6
Jones, Wali, 30, 37
Jordan, Michael, 12, 17, 18,
    29, 36

K

Karl, George, 37
Kennedy, John F., 39
Kentucky, 11
Kosloff, Irv, 12

L

Lincoln, Abraham, 17
Los Angeles Lakers, 5, 6,
    29, 33

M

Malone, Moses, 6, 9, 17,
    19–21, 27
Mount Rushmore, 17

N

New Jersey Nets, 18
North Carolina, University of, 9, 27, 35, 36

O

Overbrook (Philadelphia) High School, 14

P

Philadelphia Spectrum, 5, 29
Philadelphia Warriors, 11, 15
Phoenix Suns, 21
Portland Trail Blazers, 18

R

Richman, Isaac, 12
Ripken, Cal, Jr., 12
Roosevelt, Theodore, 17
Russell, Bill, 30

S

San Francisco Warriors, 12, 15
Schayes, Dolph, 9, 12, 15
Seattle SuperSonics, 37
Smith, Dean, 27
South Dakota, 17
Stackhouse, Jerry, 35–36
Syracuse Nationals, 12

T

Toney, Andrew, 6

V

Villanova University, 11

W

Walker, Chet, 30
Washington, George, 17
Williams, Pat, 18

WHERE TO WRITE

Philadelphia 76ers
CoreStates Center
1 CoreStates Complex
Philadelphia, PA 19148

WEBSITE

http://www.nba.com/sixers/